Next Generation ENERGY

BURNING OUT

Energy from Fossil Fuels

Nancy Dickmann

CRABTREE
Publishing Company
www.crabtreebooks.com

Crabtree Publishing Company

www.crabtreebooks.com

Author: Nancy Dickmann

Editors: Sarah Eason and Jennifer Sanderson and Petrice Custance

Proofreader: Katie Dicker

Editorial director: Kathy Middleton

Design: Paul Myerscough and Jessica Moon

Cover design: Paul Myerscough

Photo research: Sarah Eason and Jennifer Sanderson

Prepress technician: Tammy McGarr

Print coordinator: Margaret Amy Salter

Consultant: Richard Spilsbury, degree in Zoology, author and editor of educational science books for 30 years

Production coordinated by Calcium Creative

Photo Credits:

t=Top, bl=Bottom Left, br=Bottom Right

Dreamstime: Numskyman: p. 1; Shutterstock: 2xSamara.com: p. 28; A Katz: p. 13; Alberto Loyo: p. 23; Amnarj Tanongrattana: pp. 16–17; Andrei Orlov: p. 26; Andrew Zarivny: p. 27; Branislavpudar: p. 17; D. Czarnota: pp. 26–27, 30–31; Darren Brode: p. 24; Denis Burdin: pp. 20–21; Eduardo Rivero: p. 11; Everett Historical: p. 9; Gabriel12: p. 7; Hiroshi Teshigawara: p. 6; Hywit Dimyadi: p. 19; Imantsu: pp. 12–13; Irina Borsuchenko: pp. 24–25; Kris Grabiec: p. 15; Kustov: p. 8; Kzenon: p. 16; Lakeview Images: pp. 8–9; Leungchopan: p. 18; LovePHY: pp. 3, 10–11; Marcio Jose Bastos Silva: pp. 4–5; Maridav: p. 5; Mrs Ya: p. 22; Outdoorsman: pp. 14–15; Piotr Krzeslak: p. 21; Project1photography: pp. 1, 10; QiuJu Song: pp. 6–7, 32; Rena Schild: p. 20; Tigergallery: pp. 22–23; Tolga Tezcan: pp. 3br, 14; Yeamake: p. 12; Zhangyang13576997233: pp. 18–19, 28–29; Zorandim: p. 25.

Cover, p. 1: Dreamstime: Numskyman.

Cover and title page image: A gas flare stack, shown here on an offshore oil rig platform, is a device that burns off excess or waste gases.

Library and Archives Canada Cataloguing in Publication

Dickmann, Nancy, author
      Burning out : energy from fossil fuels / Nancy Dickmann.

(Next generation energy)
Includes index.
Issued in print and electronic formats.
ISBN 978-0-7787-2372-1 (bound).--
ISBN 978-0-7787-2383-7 (paperback).--
ISBN 978-1-4271-1756-4 (html)

      1. Fossil fuels--Juvenile literature. 2. Fossil fuels--
Environmental aspects--Juvenile literature. 3. Pollution--
Environmental aspects--Juvenile literature. 4. Climatic changes--
Juvenile literature. I. Title.

TP318.3.D53 2016   j333.8'2   C2015-907823-7
                                            C2015-907824-5

Library of Congress Cataloging-in-Publication Data

Names: Dickmann, Nancy, author.
Title: Burning out : energy from fossil fuels / Nancy Dickmann.
Description: Crabtree Publishing Company, [2016] | Series: Next generation energy | Includes index. | Description based on print version record and CIP data provided by publisher; resource not viewed.
Identifiers: LCCN 2015045110 (print) | LCCN 2015044044 (ebook) | ISBN 9781427117564 (electronic HTML) | ISBN 9780778723721 (reinforced library binding : alk. paper) | ISBN 9780778723837 (pbk. : alk. paper)
Subjects: LCSH: Fossil fuels--Juvenile literature. | Fossil fuels--Environmental aspects--Juvenile literature. | Pollution--Environmental aspects--Juvenile literature. | Climatic changes--Juvenile literature.
Classification: LCC TP318.3 (print) | LCC TP318.3 .D53 2016 (ebook) | DDC 333.8/2--dc23
LC record available at http://lccn.loc.gov/2015045110

Crabtree Publishing Company

www.crabtreebooks.com   1-800-387-7650

Printed in Canada/012016/BF20151123

Published in Canada
Crabtree Publishing
616 Welland Ave.
St. Catharines, Ontario
L2M 5V6

Published in the United States
Crabtree Publishing
PMB 59051
350 Fifth Avenue, 59th Floor
New York, New York 10118

Published in the United Kingdom
Crabtree Publishing
Maritime House
Basin Road North, Hove
BN41 1WR

Published in Australia
Crabtree Publishing
3 Charles Street
Coburg North
VIC, 3058

Contents

We Need Energy

Energy is the ability to do work. It comes in different forms, such as heat, light, or kinetic (movement) energy. Energy can also be passed from one object to another. For example, an apple contains sugars, which are forms of chemical energy. When you eat the apple, the chemical energy is transferred to your body. You can use it to power your muscles to swing your leg. When your leg kicks a ball, it transfers kinetic energy from you to the ball.

We use energy all the time in our daily lives. We get energy from food. We also release energy by burning **fuels**, such as gasoline and natural gas. The energy we use comes from many different sources. Some of these sources are more **sustainable**, or efficient to use, than others. **Renewable** energy is energy from a source, such as the Sun or wind, which will never run out.

However, most of the energy we use comes from sources that are nonrenewable, so they cannot be replaced. We burn huge amounts of fuels, such as **coal**, **oil**, and natural gas to power our cars and heat our homes. These resources are **extracted** from beneath the ground. Once these fuels are burned, they cannot be used again. Eventually there will be no more left.

Coal, oil, and natural gas make up the biggest "slices" of this pie, which shows the different kinds of energy used around the world.

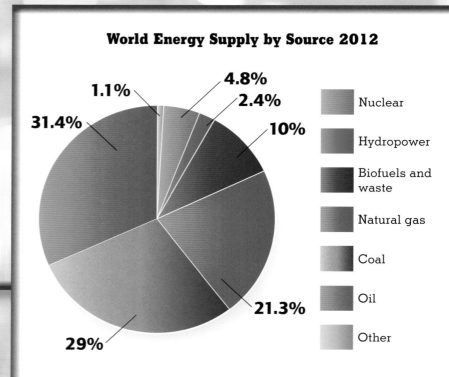

World Energy Supply by Source 2012

1.1%
4.8%
2.4%
31.4%
10%
21.3%
29%

- Nuclear
- Hydropower
- Biofuels and waste
- Natural gas
- Coal
- Oil
- Other

More and More

The world's population is growing. Currently, there are more than 7 billion people on Earth. That number will probably reach 9.7 billion in about 25 years. Not only will there be more people using energy, but they are also likely to use more of it. Our busy, modern lives use up energy at an amazing rate. One of the biggest challenges for the future is finding a way to meet these growing energy needs.

Electricity powers a huge range of devices, from streetlights to smartphones.

REWIND

Just 200 years ago, no one had electricity in their home or a car to drive from place to place. People burned wood or coal to cook their food and heat their homes. Candles and simple oil lamps provided light. Transportation was by foot, boat, or horse. The world is very different now, and we have become dependent on energy for even the simplest tasks. In what ways is daily life different, now that energy is so readily available?

What Are Fossil Fuels?

Fossil fuels are substances such as coal, oil (also called petroleum or crude oil), and natural gas, which can all be burned as fuel. Fossil fuels are found in deposits deep underground and the name provides a clue about how they got there. These kinds of fuels are formed from the remains of living things that died hundreds of millions of years ago.

When plants and animals died, their remains broke down and eventually became buried under layers of mud, rock, and sand. In some places, tons of heavy earth covered the remains, pressing down on them. All this **pressure** created a lot of heat. Over millions of years, the heat and pressure changed the plant and animal remains into fossil fuels.

Coal was formed from dead plants, such as trees and ferns. Oil and gas were formed from **microscopic** marine plants and animals, whose remains were buried at the bottom of rivers and oceans. Once the oil and natural gas were formed, they began working their way up through Earth's crust. When they ran into layers of rock too dense to seep through, they collected in pools called deposits.

In some places, petroleum seeps naturally up to the surface, where it can be seen.

Why Fossil Fuels Contain Energy

A plant uses sunlight and water to make food for itself. This food is a form of chemical energy. When an animal, such as a mouse, eats the plant, it takes in this energy. The mouse's own body stores energy that can then be passed on to a larger animal, such as an owl, when it eats the mouse. If a plant or animal dies without being eaten, the energy remains in their body. Over time, it can form a fossil fuel.

The **peat** in this bog could turn into coal in millions of years if it is buried in hot, high-pressure conditions.

FAST FORWARD

New deposits of fossil fuels are still being formed. However, the process is so slow that it will take millions of years before they are usable as fuel. One of the first stages in the formation of coal is peat. Peat is a type of wet, thick soil that is made up of decaying plants. It is found on Earth's surface in swampy environments all over the world. It builds up slowly at fewer than 0.08 inches (2 mm) per year, but it cannot start turning into coal until it is buried beneath approximately 330 to 1,300 feet (100 to 400 m) of **sediment**. That will take a very long time! What do you think might replace coal as an energy source when supplies run out?

Mining Coal

Humans have known about coal's usefulness as a fuel for thousands of years. There is evidence that coal was mined in ancient China and Greece, as well as by the Romans. These ancient peoples used coal for heating homes and other buildings. Later, during the **Industrial Revolution,** coal was used to heat the water that powered steam engines.

The first coal mines were created when people found coal on Earth's surface or very close to it, and then followed the **seam** underground. Today, mining coal is a huge, worldwide industry that uses heavy machinery for digging.

How Coal Mining Works

Coal is mined in two different ways: opencast (or surface) mining and underground (or deep) mining. In opencast mining, workers use explosives, **draglines**, and large shovels to remove the earth on top of a coal seam. Once the seam is exposed, it can be drilled and mined. Opencast mining can extract more coal than underground mining, but it can be used only when the coal seam is near the surface.

Opencast coal mines can cover an area of several square miles (or sq km). Some of the world's largest industrial equipment is used for opencast mining.

In underground coal mining, miners must dig deep to find the coal. Sometimes, the coal is mined by cutting a network of "rooms" into the coal seam. The miners leave large pillars of coal in place to support the roof. Sometimes, they are able to remove and process these pillars later. Another method used underground involves exposing large surfaces of coal, up to 1,148 feet (350 m) wide. The coal is removed in slices that range from 2 to 3.9 feet (0.6 to 1.2 m) thick.

No matter how it is mined, coal must be processed, or changed, before it can be used. Most coal is crushed, and it is often also washed in water or chemicals to remove **impurities**, such as **sulfur**.

In the past, working in a coal mine was hot, dusty, and dangerous work. For many people, however, it was the only way to support their families.

REWIND

Coal mining is a dangerous job. In the past, even young children worked in the mines. In the last century, more than 100,000 miners lost their lives in the United States alone. Mine owners wanted to keep costs low. This meant that safety sometimes suffered. Improved safety regulations mean that coal mining is safer today, but there are still occasional accidents. Do you think people would be willing to pay more for their energy if they knew that their money paid for safer working conditions for miners? Give reasons for your answer.

Drilling for Oil

Oil is found deep underground. Once a deposit is found, the oil must be extracted and then **refined** into usable products. To drill oil on land, the crew starts by drilling the main hole. The pipe stops just above where the crew thinks the oil is located. This could be many feet underground. The workers line the hole with a concrete casing to strengthen it and keep it from collapsing.

After more tests to measure the location and pressure of the oil deposit, the crew carefully drills down to the final depth. The crew uses special tools to make holes in the pipe. The oil can flow through these holes and then up the pipe. On the surface, a pump with an electric motor is attached to the head, or top, of the oil well. When it pumps up and down, it creates suction. This pulls the oil up through the well.

New technology means that oil rigs can now be built at sea to take advantage of petroleum deposits beneath the seabed.

Using the Oil

The oil that comes out of the ground often contains other substances such as sulfur or nitrogen, which might damage machinery. The oil has to be refined to remove these impurities before it can be used. This happens at a factory called a refinery.

At the refinery, the oil is heated to about 662° Fahrenheit (350° C) and pumped into a tall tank called a fractionating tower. Inside this tower are trays with holes in them. Now in vapor form, the oil rises up the tower and through the trays. When it cools, it **condenses** back into several different liquids. Heavy liquids, such as waxes, fall down to the bottom of the tower. Lighter ones, such as kerosene, stay near the top. Some of the heavier liquids can be refined further to make gasoline.

Before drilling for oil was possible, people used whale oil instead. Whale species like the right whale were nearly wiped out by whalers.

REWIND

Long ago, before drilling for oil and gas was common, many people used whale oil as a fuel. This came from the blubber, or fat, of whales. Huge numbers of whales were killed for their oil, and populations declined. Lamps fueled by whale oil were smelly, so eventually, cheaper and more efficient petroleum products were used instead. Whaling was banned in 1986 to protect the animals, although some countries refused to stop. Do you think that drilling for petroleum will ever be banned? Explain your answers.

Extracting Natural Gas

The same natural processes that produce oil also produce natural gas. These two resources are often found together, although natural gas is often formed deeper underground. Pressure deep underground forces the oil and gas to seep upward until they reach a layer of rock too dense to travel through. They remain trapped in these deposits until drilling brings them to the surface.

Deposits of natural gas are often found trapped in deep formations of a rock called **shale**. These **reservoirs**, or pools, are often 5,000 feet (1.5 km) or more below the surface, so drilling down to reach them is a difficult job. It can involve drilling through **aquifers**, where fresh water is stored underground. Drillers must be careful not to contaminate, or pollute, the aquifers.

A hole is drilled deep into the ground. Once it reaches below the deepest aquifer, the drill pipe is removed and the hole is reinforced with layers of steel, cement, and mud. The bottom part of the pipe that reaches the gas deposit has small holes punched in it. These holes allow the gas to enter the pipe and travel upward to be collected.

Once it is extracted, natural gas is often sent where it is needed through long **pipelines**.

Fracking

Some natural gas is trapped in tiny bubbles within rock. This gas cannot be extracted in the normal way. However, a new technique has allowed companies to reach it. It is called **fracking**, which is short for "hydraulic fracturing." A well is drilled deep underground, and a pipe is inserted. Instead of traveling straight down, the pipe turns at a right angle and continues traveling across. High-pressure liquid is forced through the pipe into the surrounding rock. It fractures the rock, allowing the bubbles of gas to escape. Fracking has allowed companies to extract gas from deposits that could not be reached in the past.

Many people want to ban fracking. It uses a lot of water, and there are concerns that it can trigger earthquakes and pollute aquifers.

The Energy Future: You Choose

Fracking has increased natural gas production. This has led to a drop in the price of natural gas, which is good for the consumers. Fracking also helps countries like the United States become less dependent on fossil fuels imported from other countries. Are these benefits worth the environmental harm many believe it causes? Explain your answer.

Where in the World?

Fossil fuels are used all over the world, but deposits are found only in certain places. Their underground locations mean that they are not always easy to find. Energy companies spend huge amounts of money searching for new deposits of fossil fuels, especially oil and natural gas.

Deposits of coal are found in almost every country. However, some of these deposits are in places that would make them very difficult to mine. In some cases, the cost of getting the coal out of the ground would be more than the coal is worth. Even so, there are more than 70 countries that have deposits that can be mined. The biggest deposits are in China, the United States, India, Australia, and South Africa.

Oil and natural gas deposits are rarer. The top five oil producers are the United States, Saudi Arabia, Russia, China, and Canada. The top 15 oil-producing countries also include Kuwait, Brazil, and Venezuela. Many of the same countries also appear on the list of top natural gas producers. Russia, the United States, and Canada take the top three spots.

To get it where it is needed, oil is often shipped long distances in enormous tankers.

Fossil Fuels and Politics

Fossil fuels are so important to most countries that making sure they have a steady supply is crucial. They are also important to the world economy, so countries with large deposits often have more political influence. Some countries sign deals with oil-rich countries, and trade political favors to get drilling licenses in that country. Sometimes, countries withhold exports of fossil fuels to force other countries to act in a certain way.

Drilling in the Arctic region would disturb the feeding ground for large animals such as walruses, polar bears, seals, and whales, as well as fish and microscopic creatures.

The Energy Future: You Choose

There are huge deposits of oil and natural gas in the Arctic, mostly deep under the seabed. Scientists estimate that this region holds the world's largest untapped gas deposits, and some of the biggest remaining oil deposits, too. However, there are concerns that oil and gas drilling could harm the important **ecosystems** of the Arctic Ocean. Some locations are protected from drilling, but that may change. Does our need for oil and gas outweigh our responsibility to protect the environment? Explain your answer.

How We Use Fossil Fuels

In the United States, about 75 percent of the energy consumed comes from fossil fuels. They have a huge range of uses. You probably already know that people depend on them to fuel their cars and heat their homes. You may not realize that fossil fuels are also used in the manufacturing of many familiar products, or that they produce some of our electricity.

Transportation makes up a huge chunk of energy usage. In Canada, it accounts for 34 percent of all energy use. This includes gasoline for cars and motorcycles; diesel fuel for buses, trucks, and trains; and kerosene for airplanes. Fossil fuels are widely used to heat homes and businesses. Coal fires were common until natural gas became more popular. Now, many homes are heated by electricity. In Canada, most of that electricity is produced through **hydroelectric power**, but some is generated by burning fossil fuels. We often use natural gas in our stoves, and some of the machines in our factories are powered by fossil fuels.

In the United States, oil accounts for 89 percent of all fuel used for transportation. The gasoline used in cars is just one of the products made from oil.

Plastic and Other Products

Fossil fuels are a key ingredient in many familiar products, from medicines and cosmetics to lubricants (grease or oils) and **synthetic** (human-made) fabrics. One of their biggest uses is in the manufacturing of plastics. Familiar substances such as polyester, nylon, polystyrene, vinyl, Lycra, silicone, and Teflon are all types of plastic. Some of the earliest plastics were made from coal products. However, since the 1950s, most have been made from petroleum products instead. Plastics are everywhere: in our clothes and cars, in our gadgets, in food packaging, and many more.

Factories churn out millions of items, either made from plastic or packaged in plastic.

REWIND

We are so used to plastic that it is hard to picture a world without it. However, even just 100 years ago, synthetic plastics were still fairly rare. Instead of being sold in plastic bottles, shampoo came in glass bottles. Toothpaste tubes were made of metal, and shopping was carried in a reusable basket or paper bags. Much of today's packaging is made from plastic. Do you think this will change in the future, when fossil fuels are nearly gone? Give reasons for your answer.

Electricity from Fossil Fuels

Oil, coal, and natural gas can all be burned in power plants to generate electricity. No matter what type of fuel is used, the process works in more or less the same way. Even **nuclear power** stations, which create heat using chemical reactions instead of burning fuel, follow the same basic principles.

The first step is burning the fuel in a giant **furnace**. This releases the heat energy that is stored in the fuel. Heat from the furnace flows around pipes filled with cold water in a piece of equipment called a boiler. The heat boils the water and turns it into steam. Then the steam is pumped to a **turbine**, which is a rotating wheel with blades. The steam's force makes the turbine's blades spin.

The turbine is linked to a machine called a **generator**. The generator is able to convert kinetic energy, created by the movement of the blades, into electrical energy. This electricity is then increased to a very high **voltage** and sent out over wires or cables to where it is needed.

The chimneys and cooling towers of power plants that burn fossil fuels are a familiar sight in many places.

Good or Bad?

Each type of fuel has its own benefits and disadvantages. Coal is cheap and easily available, but burning it in power stations uses up a lot of water and creates **pollution**. Burning oil produces less **carbon dioxide** and it uses less water. Natural gas is the cleanest of the fossil fuels. It burns efficiently and releases less carbon dioxide than either oil or coal. New technologies for extracting natural gas, such as fracking, have increased the amount that can be collected lowering its price. However, it is still far from perfect.

The turbines in a power station are a little like windmills, but with many more blades. The steam pushes against these blades to make the turbines spin.

FAST FORWARD

Engineers are looking at new ways to generate electricity, preparing for a day when fossil fuels are no longer available. Renewable energy sources like solar, wind, and hydroelectric power (power from moving water) are slowly becoming more widespread and cost-effective. However, they are a long way from taking over from fossil fuels. In the United States, burning fossil fuels produces nearly 70 percent of electricity. Why do you think 70 percent of electricity is still created by burning fossil fuels? Explain your answer.

Climate Change

We depend on fossil fuels for many things. Transportation, heating, manufacturing, and electricity are just a few. However, our dependence on fossil fuels is harming the planet. Burning these fuels releases gases into the air, and these often invisible gases can have a huge effect on Earth.

A layer of gases, called the atmosphere, surrounds Earth. The atmosphere helps hold some of the Sun's heat, making the planet warm enough to live on. It also protects the planet from some types of harmful **radiation**. However, when **greenhouse gases**, such as carbon dioxide and methane, build up in the atmosphere, they keep heat from escaping back into space. This causes an increase in Earth's average temperature.

The biggest source of human-produced greenhouse gases is the burning of fossil fuels, which releases carbon dioxide into the atmosphere. In Canada, 25 percent of greenhouse gas emissions are produced by the oil and gas industry. Transportation is just behind, at 23 percent, and most of this is produced by burning oil as fuel.

It's time to cut carbon

Many people are pressuring governments to pass laws that will restrict or reduce greenhouse gas emissions.

Problems with Warming

Scientists estimate that the average temperature on Earth has risen by about 1.3° Fahrenheit (0.7° C) in the last 100 years. Predictions for the next century range from a 2° Fahrenheit (1.1° C) rise to an 11.5° Fahrenheit (6.4° C) rise. Higher temperatures could mean big changes. They could make ice caps and glaciers melt, causing sea levels to rise. Millions of people living in low-lying areas could be **displaced** if their homes flood. The temperatures could also disrupt ocean currents such as the Gulf Stream, which helps keep parts of Europe warm. Weather patterns could change, with more frequent droughts and storms, and animals and plants could find it harder to survive in a warmer environment.

The warming of the planet from carbon dioxide trapped in the atmosphere is called the greenhouse effect. Trees and other plants combat the effect because they absorb carbon dioxide. Unfortunately, Earth's forests are being cut down. When trees are burned, they release even more carbon dioxide.

REWIND

Volcanic eruptions spew ash into the air, which reflects sunlight away from Earth. The ash from a very large eruption can cool the planet by 1.8° Fahrenheit (1° C) for a year or more. This happened after the eruption of Mount Tambora in Indonesia in 1815. Even this small change had a big impact. The cooler temperatures made crops fail and food prices rise. What do you think might happen if Earth's temperature rises by a few degrees over a few years? Explain your answer.

Pollution and Other Problems

Fossil fuels can cause problems at any stage: when they are extracted, processed, transported, and burned. One of the biggest problems is that they are nonrenewable. We are slowly but surely using up the world's supply of fossil fuels. Once they are gone, we cannot make more.

Burning fossil fuels releases carbon dioxide into the air. The process also releases other gases that pollute the air. These include carbon monoxide, nitrogen oxides, sulfur oxides, and hydrocarbons. Burning fossil fuels also releases tiny particles of solid matter such as soot and smoke. Some of these substances mix with fog forming a thick haze called smog. Some mix with water vapor producing acid rain. The gases and particles can also cause breathing difficulties and other health problems for many living things.

Oil spills can harm animals such as seabirds. Their feathers lose their waterproof properties when coated by oil.

Mining and Drilling

Extracting fossil fuels comes with its own problems. Coal mines and oil-and-gas-drilling operations can destroy **habitats**, causing problems for the plants and animals that live there. When water washes through coal mines, it mixes with a substance called pyrite. Pyrite pollutes rivers and streams. Even when a mine is closed and covered over, the soil above it can still end up being less productive.

Another problem is the risk of disasters, which can kill people as well as harm the environment. In particular, working with oil and gas carries the risk of fire or explosion. For example, in 2010, the Deepwater Horizon oil rig was sunk by an explosion. Eleven workers died and around 5 million barrels of oil were spilled into the Gulf of Mexico. Spills can also happen when oil is transported along pipelines or in huge ships.

Many oil pipelines go through wilderness areas. Important habitats can be destroyed when they are built, and the pipelines can get in the way of animals as they move around.

The Energy Future: You Choose

Engineers are working on ways to make fossil fuels cleaner and safer. For example, one company has developed a way to capture carbon dioxide and pollutants from coal or gas-fired power plants. These substances can be turned into concrete for use in buildings. Even if we make fossil fuels cleaner to burn, it does not change the fact that they will eventually run out. Do you think scientists should focus on finding alternative energy sources instead? Explain your answer.

The Case for Fossil Fuels

In spite of the problems with fossil fuels, they are still the most widely used energy source. There are several good reasons why we are so dependent on fossil fuels. Here are a few of them:

Cost: For now, fossil fuels are fairly cheap and plentiful. However, prices will likely go up in the near future. We are using up Earth's supply of easily extracted fossil fuels, and it costs more to extract the harder-to-reach ones. Oil and natural gas are running out faster than coal.

Efficiency: Fossil fuels are efficient. This means that burning a relatively small amount of fuel will release a lot of energy.

Ease of use: The technology to extract, refine, and use fossil fuels is tried and tested. Many common machines, including cars, have been designed to run on fossil fuels.

Electric cars are an alternative to gasoline-powered cars. For many years, it was difficult to recharge them, but charging stations are much more common today.

Reliability: Using fossil fuels does not depend on conditions like the weather. This gives fossil fuels an advantage over wind and solar power, which can be harnessed only at certain times.

Location: Coal is found in a wide range of locations. Even oil and natural gas, which are only found in certain locations, are easy to transport, so they can be used anywhere.

Helping the economy: Extracting and refining fossil fuels is a huge industry that provides jobs for millions of people around the world. Selling fossil fuels to other countries has made some nations very rich.

Useful products: Refining fossil fuels produces useful materials such as plastics. These materials are then used to make countless products.

Drilling for oil provides many people with employment. This means that it also boosts the country's economy.

The Energy Future: You Choose

Fossil fuels have benefits as well as disadvantages. When a new deposit of coal, oil, or gas is found, the government must often decide if the benefits of extracting it outweigh the potential harm it could cause. For example, a shale gas well could provide jobs for the local community, but it could also use up precious water resources and harm wildlife. Do you think you would support a company's proposal to open a mine or well in your local area? Why or why not?

What Is the Alternative?

We need to reduce our dependence on fossil fuels because they will run out at some point in the near future. Kicking the fossil fuel habit now will help protect the planet. Luckily, there are more sustainable alternatives. Here are just a few:

Solar power: Solar panels absorb energy from the Sun's rays and convert it into other types of energy. Some types of solar panels turn sunlight into electricity. Others gather heat energy from the Sun and use it to heat water or other liquids.

Wind power: Tall wind turbines spin in the wind and convert this motion into electricity. The turbines are efficient only if placed in the right location. Some wind farms are out at sea, where winds are stronger and more reliable.

Hydroelectric power: The energy in moving water can be used to spin turbines and generate electricity. This can be done in a river or by using the power of waves or tides.

Nuclear power: A chemical process known as nuclear fission releases a huge amount of energy that is used in power plants to generate electricity. Though this is a more sustainable form of energy, nuclear power is not completely renewable.

Solar panels are becoming a common sight, either on roofs or as part of large solar farms like this one.

This is because a nuclear power plant uses uranium, which is not a renewable resource.

Biomass energy: Biomass is any plant or animal remains or products that are burned as fuel. This includes wood, straw, and methane, a gas that can be produced from cow manure.

Geothermal power: This type of energy uses heat from below the ground. The deeper underground you go, the hotter it gets. We can harness this energy to generate electricity or to keep homes warm.

The dams used to create hydroelectric power can produce a huge amount of electricity. The Hoover Dam (shown above provides electricity for nearly 8 million people in Arizona, California, and Nevada.

FAST FORWARD

Scientists estimate that about 21 percent of the world's electricity is generated by the renewable sources listed here. When you add nuclear, which is not truly renewable, the total goes up to 32 percent. This percentage is expected to rise over the upcoming decades. However, the renewable share of total energy usage is much smaller. This is because electricity is only one of the ways we use energy—for example, we cannot use solar power to fuel passenger planes. What do you think the energy landscape will look like a century from now? Explain your answer.

Power Up!

For centuries, fossil fuels have powered the planet. However, we need to reduce the amount of fossil fuels we use if we want to prevent pollution and stop climate change. There are a lot of small changes you can make in your daily life that will help cut down on your fossil fuel use. For example, walk or ride your bicycle instead of going by car for short journeys. You could also arrange to share rides to after-school activities.

What Can You Do?

Saving electricity often means saving fossil fuels, too. Turning off lights and gadgets when you are not using them is a start. Only run the dishwasher when it is full, and hang laundry outside on sunny days instead of using the dryer. You could help your parents research the cost and benefits of installing solar panels on the roof if you live in a house, or help research more energy-efficient appliances.

The energy saved by hanging just one load of laundry outside to dry would power an energy-saving light bulb for 150 hours!

Activity:

Extracting oil requires a lot of engineering know-how. Depending on the location, each oil well comes with its own challenges. Here is a simple activity that will help you understand more about how oil is extracted from deep underground.

You Will Need:

- Pair of scissors
- 8 identical drinking straws
- Masking tape
- A friend
- Glass of chocolate milk
- Chair
- Permission from an adult

drinking straw

masking tape

glass

Instructions

1. Cut a short slit in the end of one straw. Push this end inside the end of another straw.
2. Wrap masking tape around the place where the two straws join, making an airtight seal.
3. In the same way, cut a slit in each of the other straws and attach them, one by one, to make a long tube. Seal each joint with masking tape.
4. Ask a friend to hold the glass of milk steadily on the floor. This is your oil. Climb up on the chair and put one end of your pipe into the drink. This is your oil well.
5. Put the other end of the pipe in your mouth. Try to suck up some of the liquid. Is it difficult?
6. Cut one straw off the tube and try again. Is it a bit easier now?
7. Continue to cut off the straws, one at a time. Which length makes it easiest to drink?

What Happened?

The length of the straw affects how easy it is to suck up the liquid. The longer the straw, the harder it is to get the liquid all the way up. Some oil deposits are found very deep underground. The deeper they are, the more energy will be required to pump the oil to the surface. The viscosity, or thickness, of the oil also affects how easy it is to pump.

Glossary

Please note: Some bold-faced words are defined where they appear in the text

aquifers Layers of rock, sand, or gravel underground that contain water

carbon dioxide A gas molecule made of a carbon atom joined with two oxygen atoms

chemical energy Power created when substances react to each other

coal A hard, black substance found in the earth that can be burned as fuel

condenses Changes from a gas back into a liquid

displaced Forced from one's usual place

draglines Large digging machines that have a bucket, which is pulled in by a wire cable

ecosystems The plants, animals, and other organisms that live together in a specific environment

extracted Removed or pulled out

fracking A method of creating cracks in rock to extract natural gas that is trapped in rock

fuels Anything, such as wood or gasoline, that can be burned as a source of energy

furnace An enclosed structure that is used to heat things

generator A machine that changes movement into electrical energy

greenhouse gases Gases like carbon dioxide and methane that contribute to the greenhouse effect

habitats The places where plants or animals usually live

hydroelectric power Energy generated by moving water

impurities Substances that can mix with another substance and make it less pure

Industrial Revolution A rapid change where countries become more focused on using machines to make goods

microscopic Able to be seen only through a microscope

nuclear power A form of power generated when atoms are split to release energy

oil A thick liquid found beneath Earth's surface that can be burned for fuel. It is often called petroleum or crude oil

peat A type of wet, thick soil that is made up of decaying plants

pipelines Long lines of pipes for moving gas or oil from where it is produced to where it is used or sold

pollution Something introduced into the environment that causes harmful or poisonous effects

pressure The force produced when one thing presses or pushes against something else

radiation Waves of energy sent out by sources of heat or light, such as the Sun or by radioactive substances

refined Made pure or made into other products. Oil and gas must be refined before they can be used.

renewable Something that renews itself once it is used

reservoirs Large supplies of something

seam A long, narrow layer of coal or another mineral in Earth

sediment Material, such as sand, that is carried by water or wind and deposited somewhere else

shale A type of rock made of many thin layers that can be split into sheets

sulfur A solid, nonmetallic chemical element that is tasteless, odorless, brittle, and pale yellow in color

sustainable Done in a way that conserves and efficiently uses resources

synthetic Made by humans rather than occurring naturally

turbine A machine in which a rotor is made to turn by the power of the wind, moving water, or by steam

voltage A measure of electrical force

Learning More

Find out more about fossil fuels.

Books

Einspruch, Andrew. *What Is Energy?* (Discovery Education: How It Works). PowerKids Press, 2014.

Iyer, Rani. *Endangered Energy: Investigating the Scarcity of Fossil Fuels* (Endangered Earth). Capstone Press, 2015.

Marrin, Albert. *Black Gold: The Story of Oil in Our Lives.* Knopf Books for Young Readers, 2012.

Websites

The U.S. Department of Energy's website explains how fossil fuels formed at:
www.fe.doe.gov/education/energylessons/coal/gen_howformed.html

The Energy Information Administration has lots of information about fossil fuels at:
www.eia.gov/tools/faqs/index.cfm#naturalgas

This website has a list of tips that will help you reduce your use of fossil fuels:
www.ecy.wa.gov/climatechange/whatucando.htm

Find out how oil is extracted and about the different products made from it at:
www.eia.gov/kids/energy.cfm?page=oil_home-basics

Index